Someone Loves You...

Josh Naylor

Ark House Press
PO Box 1722, Port Orchard, WA 98366 USA
PO Box 1321, Mona Vale NSW 1660 Australia
PO Box 318 334, West Harbour, Auckland 0661 New Zealand
arkhousepress.com

SOMEONE LOVES YOU!

Cataloguing in Publication Data:
SomeOne Loves You / Josh Naylor
ISBN: 9780648715092

Photography, Design and layout by Josh Naylor
Edited by Libby Volke

Dedicated to those who are suffering....

May you truly find peace and freedom in the hands of God.

If God spends so much time and energy creating detail we can't see with the naked eye....

how much more time and energy do you think God spends creating and crafting you...

'Long before He laid down earth's foundations, He had us in mind, had settled on us

as the focus of His love, to be made whole and holy by His love. Long, long ago

He decided to adopt us into His family through Jesus Christ.

(What pleasure He took in planning this!)'

Ephesians 1:4-5 (MSG)

'He had us in mind, had settled on us as the focus of His love,'

God planned, before the earth was formed, to concentrate His love on You!

He planned for His love to make you whole and not broken.

He planned to make you holy and to not be ashamed.

He planned to be your Father, through Jesus Christ!.

'Before I formed you in the womb I knew you,

before you were born I set you apart;'

Jeremiah 1:5 (NIV)

'Before I formed you in the womb I knew you,'

God knew and experienced you before you were born.

He gave you special gifts and talents that set you

apart from others.

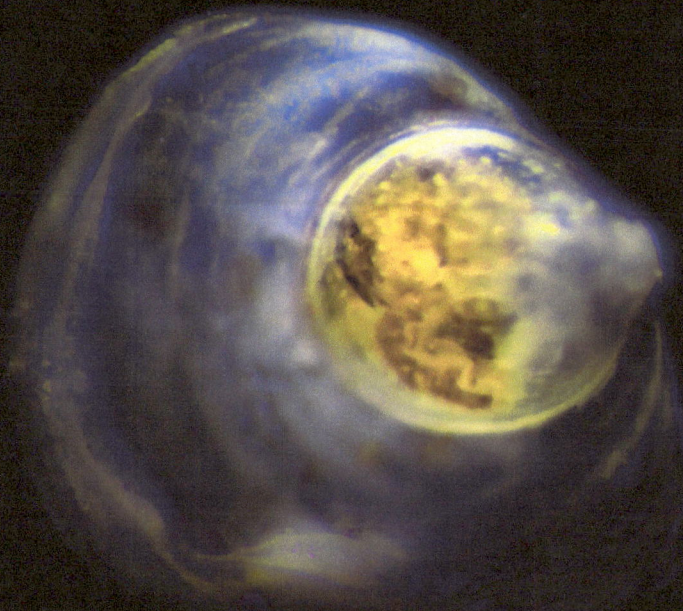

'You watched me as I was formed in utter seclusion, as I was woven together in the dark of the womb.

You saw me before I was born.

Every day of my life was recorded in Your book.

Every moment was laid out before a single day had passed.'

Psalm 139:15-16 (NLT)

'You watched me as I was formed in utter seclusion, as I was woven together in the dark...'

God knows and cares about every facet of you and He planned out

every day of your life. He also gave you the freedom to

choose. To choose to fulfill the plans He designed especially for you.

'You made all the delicate, inner parts of my body and knit me together in my mother's womb.

Thankyou for making me so wonderfully complex!

Your workmanship is marvellous - How well I know it.'

Psalm 139:13-14 (NLT)

'You made all the delicate, inner parts of my body and knit me together in my mother's womb'

You are an incredible 'work of art'.

You are intentionally created.

It took God Himself nine months to knit, craft and detail your body, character and spirit -

YOU!

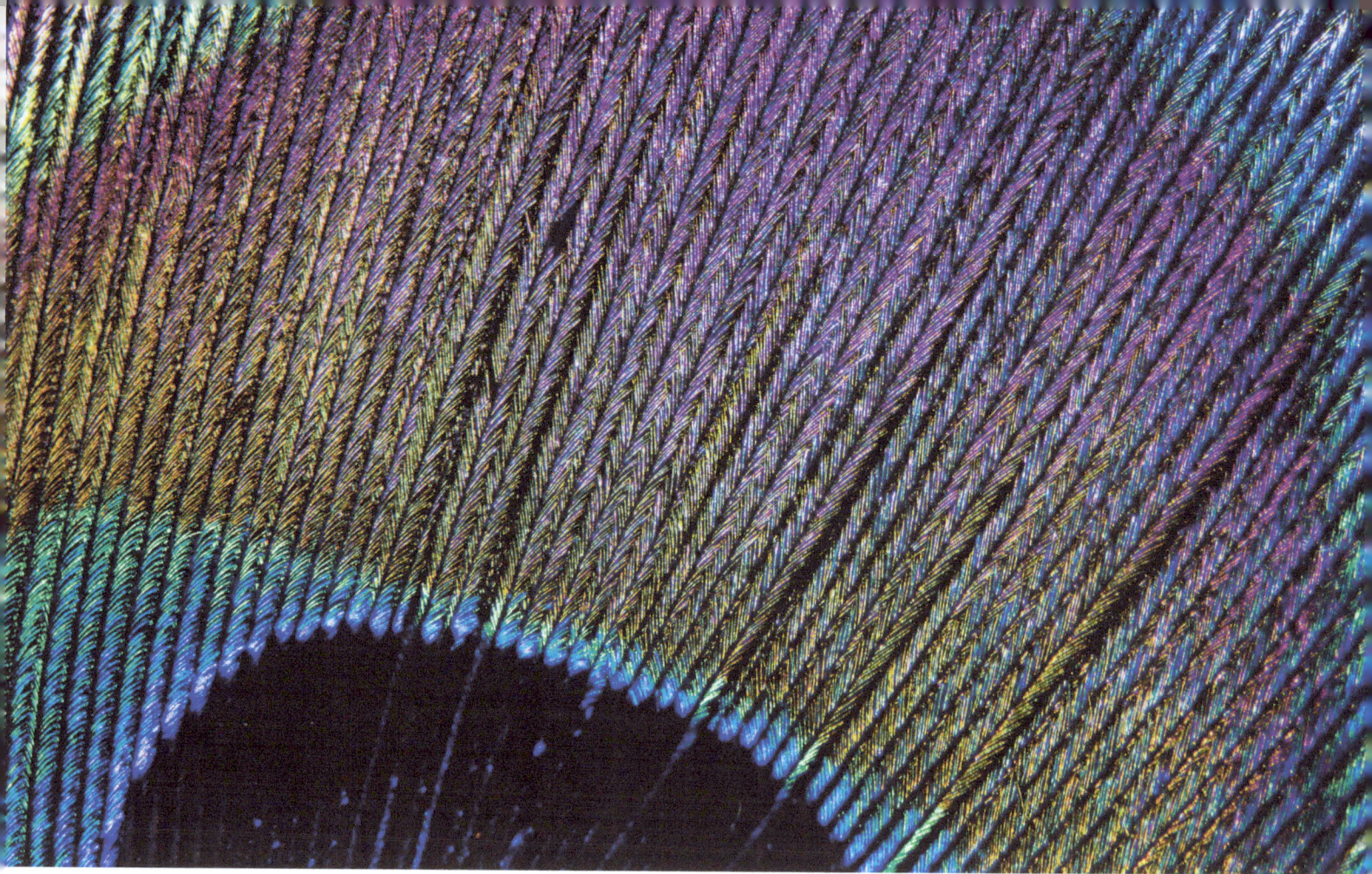

'So God created people in His own image;

God patterned them after Himself;

male and female He created them."

"Then God looked over all He had made, and He saw that it was excellent in every way.'

Genesis 1:27, 31 (NLT)

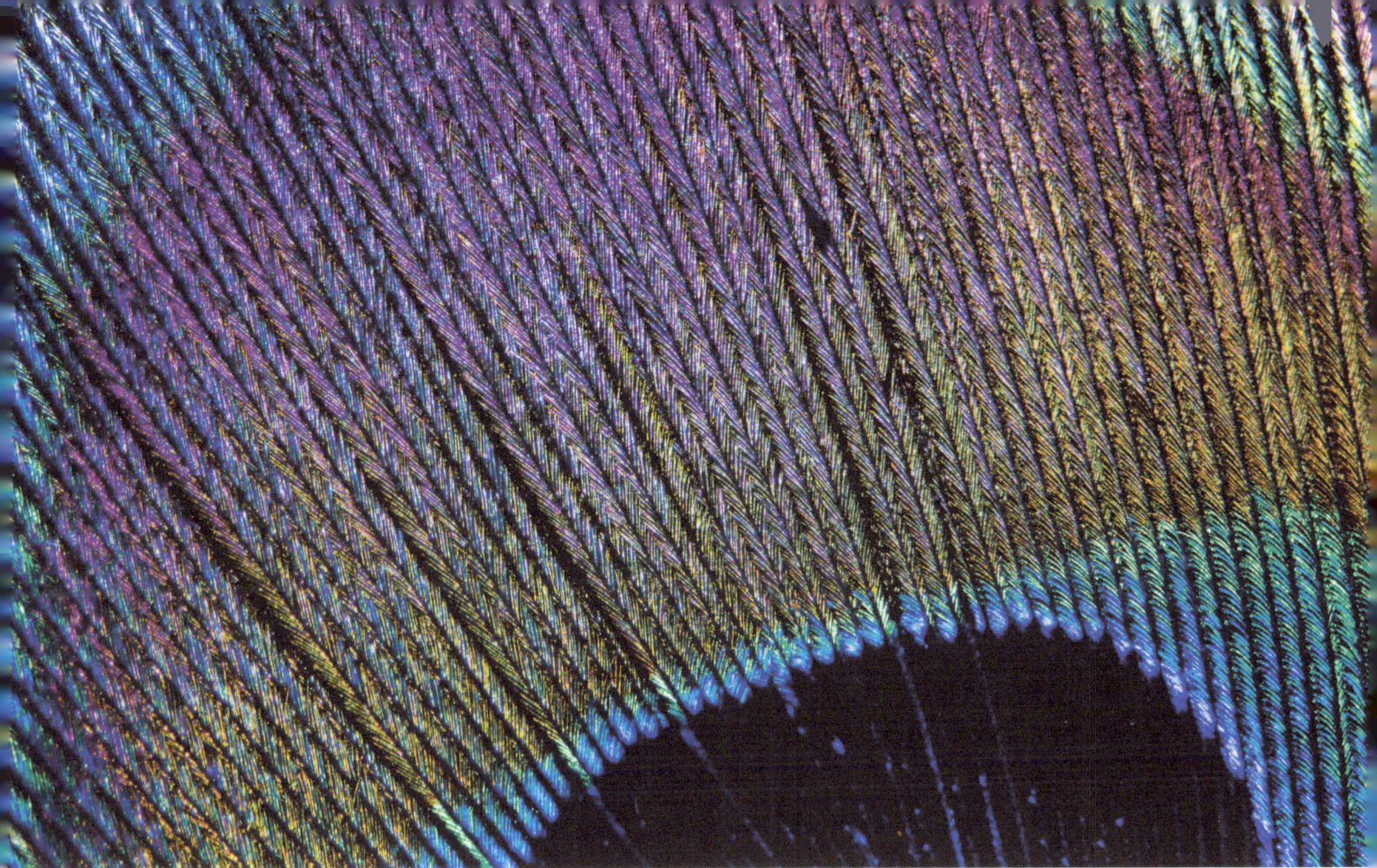

'God created people in His own image; God patterned them after Himself.'

You have been designed and created as a reflection of God Himself.

Therefore, you have inherited God's qualites of love, humility, compassion, mercy, grace,

forgiveness and truth. Explore and nurture these attiributes to enhance yourself and

bestow them on others that need them.

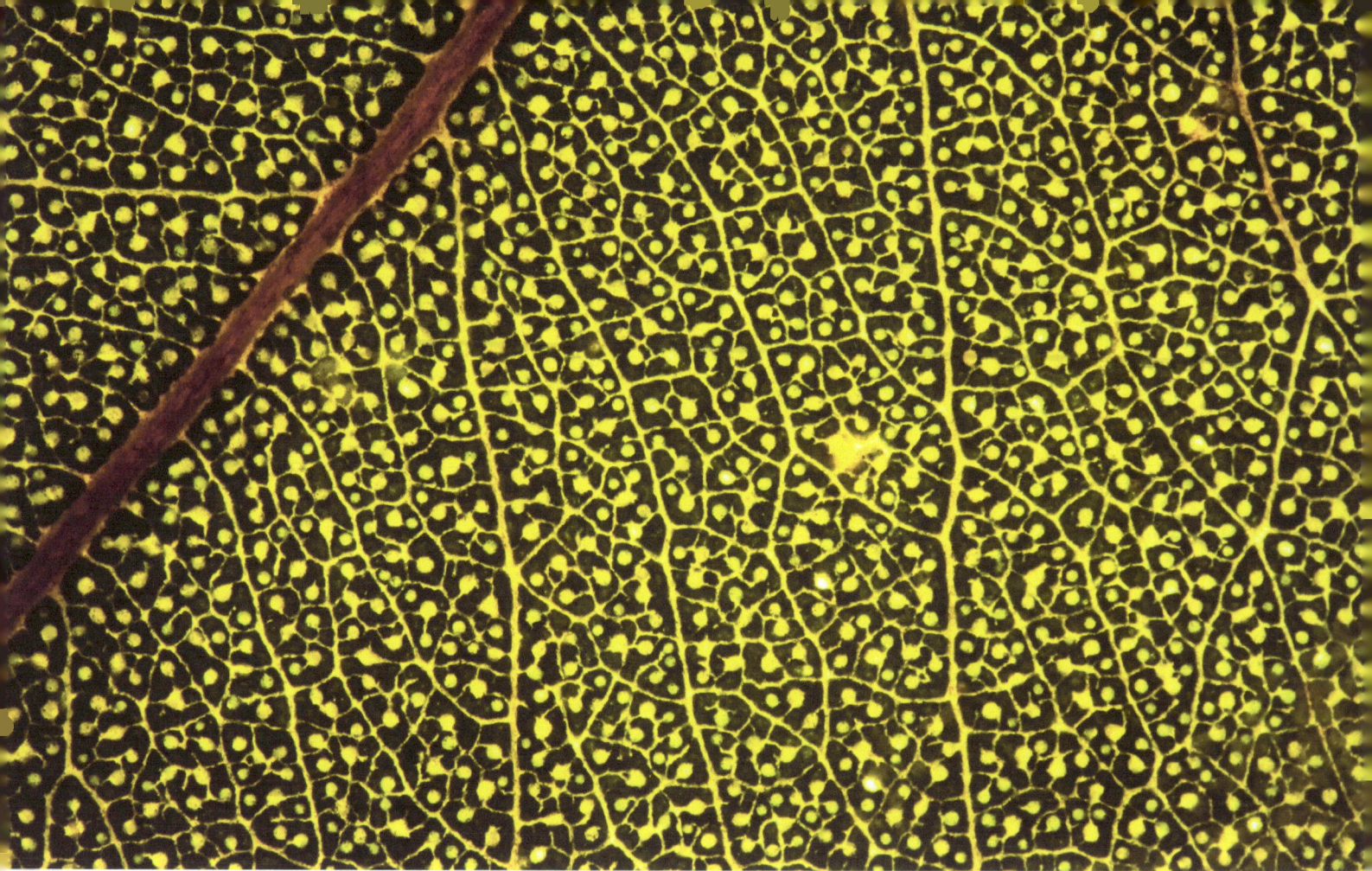

'How precious are your thoughts about me, O God. They cannot be numbered!

I can't even count them; they outnumber the grains of sand!

And when I wake up, you are still with me!'

Psalm 139:17-18 (NLT)

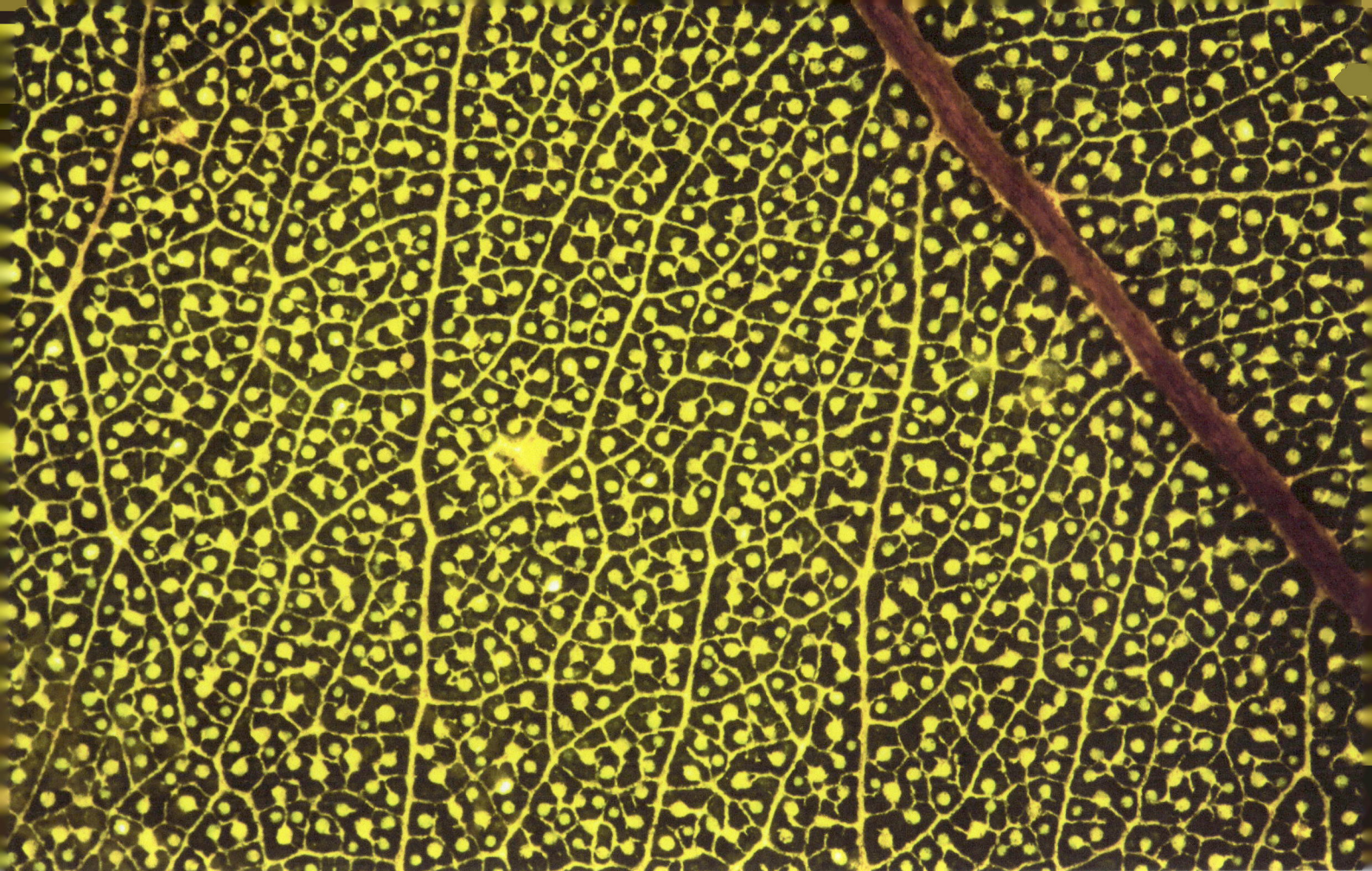

How precious are your thoughts about me, O God. They cannot be numbered!

You are forever on the mind of God.

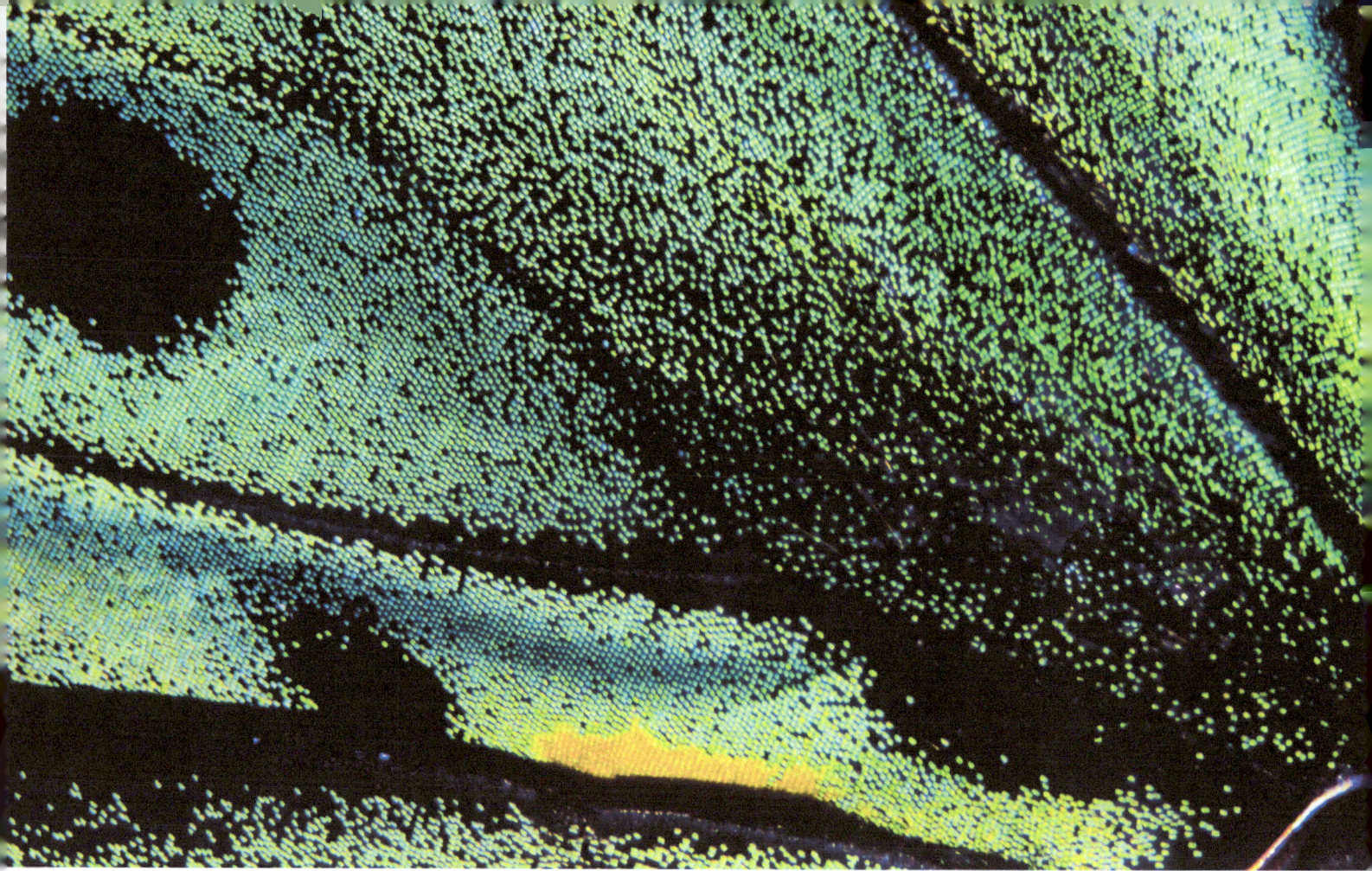

'For we are God's masterpiece. He has created us anew in Christ Jesus,

so that we can do the good things He planned for us long ago.'

Ephesians 2:10 (NLT)

'For we are God's masterpiece.'

Firstly, You are a masterpiece!

Secondly, bring your brokenness to God and He will make you whole when you

receive Jesus Christ into your life!

Thirdly, God has implanted special gifts and characteristics within you, so if you

choose, you can use them to bless others.

'God is good, a hiding place in tough times.

He recognises and welcomes anyone looking for help, no matter how desperate the trouble.'

Nahum 1:7 (MSG)

'God is good, a hiding place in tough times'

No matter what choices you have made or cirmcumstances you are going through,
God makes Himself fully available to you, with His arms outstretched ready to
embrace you and provide a space for healing.

"The Lord is compassionate and gracious, slow to anger, abounding in love.

He will not always accuse, nor will He harbor His anger forever;

He does not treat us as our sins deserve or repay us according to our iniquities.

For as high as the heavens are above the earth, so great is His love for those who fear Him;

as far as the east is from the west, so far has He removed our transgressions from us."

Psalm 103:8-12 (NIV)

'...as far as the east is from the west, so far has He removed our transgressions from us.'

God will not give up on you, even if others have. He's always at the ready to pour
forgiveness, grace and mercy on our lives. All we have to do is ask Him,
and He'll separate you from your sins and restore your life.

'Are you tired? Worn out? Burned out on religion? Come to Me.

Get away with Me and you'll recover your life. I'll show you how to take a real rest.

Walk with Me and work with Me - watch how I do it.

Learn the unforced rhythms of grace. I won't lay anything heavy or ill-fitting on you.

Keep company with Me and you'll learn to live freely and lightly.'

Matthew 11:28-30 (MSG)

'Keep company with me and you'll learn to live freely and lightly.'

If you are broken, tormented, tired, stressed or a believer in distress, Jesus Christ is reaching out, inviting you to pray and give your troubles to Him. In return, He will give you rest and peace. His calmness and grace will fall on you. Be open to Jesus and His 'ways', for He will lead you to find the solutions to your problems.

'...nothing can ever separate us from His love.

Death can't, and life can't. The angels won't, and all the powers of hell itself cannot keep God's love away. Our fears for today, our worries about tomorrow, or where we are - high above the sky, or in the deepest ocean - nothing will ever be able to separate us from the love of God demonstrated by the Lord Jesus Christ when He died for us.'

Romans 8:38-39 (TLB)

'nothing will ever be able to separate us from the love of God...'

Things you have done in past cannot separate you from God's love, nor things that
you will do in the future. People and the spiritual world cannot stop God from loving you.
God's loves you unconditionally!

'Seek the Lord while you can still find Him. Call on Him now while He is near.

Let them turn to the Lord that He may have mercy on them.

Yes, turn to our God, for He will abundantly pardon.'

Isaiah 55:6-7 (NLT)

'Yes, turn to our God, for He will abundantly pardon.'

God wants to forgive you for all the mistakes you have made, even if you have
trouble forgiving yourself. Give God permission to pour out His compassion,
forgiveness and love on your life and He will set you free from oppression,
guilt and torment

If you desire to start over a fresh, new life with God and receive His abundant forgiveness and grace, then repeat the following prayer:

Heavenly Father,

I humbly come before you, a sinner needing Your saving grace. I know I have sinned against You, but I sincerely ask for Your forgiveness. Thank You Jesus for dying for me on the Cross so I can receive eternal life with You. Cleanse and wash me clean under the redemptive blood of Jesus. I ask that You would come into my life and dwell within me. Help me to follow You. Guide me, change me, renew and strengthen me in You.

In Jesus' mighty and precious name, Amen.

Congratulations!
You are saved, reborn, and a great future awaits you!
Cultivate a relationship with Jesus by praying, studying the Bible and finding a
church community that you can feel a part of.

'...to know (to perceive, recognise, become acquainted with, and understand) You, the only true and real God,'

'And this is eternal life: [it means] to know (to perceive, recognise, become acquainted
with, and understand) You, the only true and real God, and [likewise] to know Him,
Jesus [as the] Christ (the Anointed One, the Messiah), Whom You have sent.'
John 17:3 (AMP)

May this book reveal to you how much you are loved. Remember you are never alone

and that...

Every twenty-four hours God gives us a fresh start to leave the past behind.

'...anyone who belongs to Christ has become a new person.
The old life is gone, a new life has begun!'
2 Corinthians 5:17 (NLT)

'the old life is gone, a new life has begun!'

In God's eyes, you become a new person when you give your heart to Jesus Christ.
He will free you from your past and a fresh start is readily available.

'I will be your God throughout your lifetime - until your hair is white with age.

I made you, and I will care for you. I will carry you along and save you.'

Isaiah 46:4 (NLT)

'I made you, and I will care for you.'

God is devoted to you and lives within you.

The healing has begun!

Phaleanopsis Orchid (Magnified 0.7x)

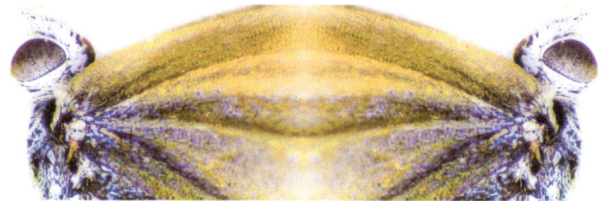
Moth   (Magnified 2.5x)

Sydney Rock Oyster Spat (Magnified 80x)

Butterfly Wing (Magnified 80x)

Peacock Feather   (Magnified 0.63x)

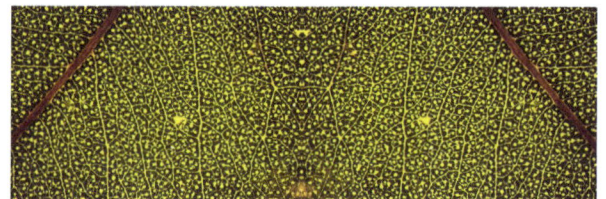
Eucalypt Leaf (Magnified 1x)

Butterfly Wing   (Magnified 0.63x)

Bug (Magnified 40x)

Cockatoo Feather   (Magnified 12.6x)

Feather   (Magnified 14x)

Grasshopper   (Magnified 38x)

Sea Urchin (Magnified 1.25x)

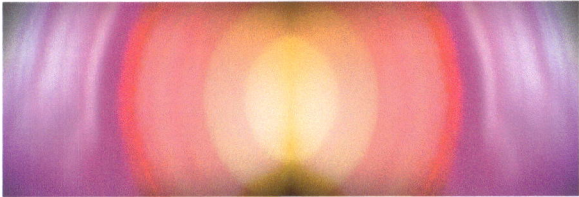
Agate   (Magnified 72x)

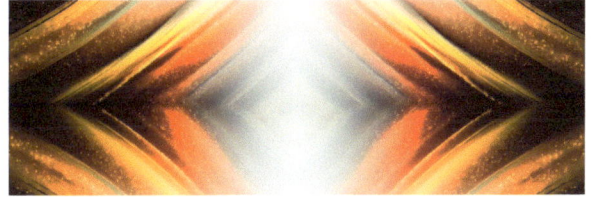
Agate   (Magnified 4x)

Strelitzia germinated seed (Magnified 0.9x)

Beetle's back (Magnified 1.6x)

www.ingramcontent.com/pod-product-compliance
Lightning Source LLC
Chambersburg PA
CBHW042003100426
42813CB00020B/2965